D1439872

For the ones they are in darkness
And the others are in light;
And you see the ones in brightness
Those in darkness drop from sight.

— Brecht

JEFFREY WAINWRIGHT

Selected Poems

Carcanet Press · Manchester

First published in 1985 by
Carcanet Press Limited
208-212 Corn Exchange Buildings
Manchester M4 3BQ

British Library Cataloguing in Publication Data
Wainwright, Jeffrey
Selected poems.
I. Title
821'.914   PR6073.A353

ISBN 0-85635-598-4

The publisher acknowledges the financial assistance
of the Arts Council of Great Britain.

Typeset by Bryan Williamson, Swinton, Berwickshire
Printed in England by SRP Ltd, Exeter

Contents

I

II

III

IV

V

For Judith

Acknowledgements

This collection contains poems that have previously been published in *The Important Man* (Northern House, 1970), and *Heart's Desire* (Carcanet, 1978).

Further acknowledgement and thanks are due as follows: for 'Transitive' to *Stand*; for 'Sea Dreams' to *Poetry Supplement* for the Poetry Book Society, Christmas 1981, reprinted in *Helix* (Australia) and *The Agni Review* (US); for 'The Mad Talk of George III and A Hymn to Liberty' to *Poetry Now* (BBC Radio 3), and *Poetry Nation Review*, reprinted *Harvard Magazine* (US) and *Some Contemporary Poets of Britain and Ireland*.

I should like to thank the Department of English and History in the Faculty of Humanities of Manchester Polytechnic for the leave during which this book was completed.

I

Transitive

in memory of Daniel Richardson

"The body makes love possible" —Galway Kinnell

This stripe of light
we lie inside,
a curtain crack,
carries me to you.
Another day,
a window breeze,
touching my shoulder, speaks
of what is realized,
like how you walk, or eat,
or dress, or sleep.
Love is made tenable
in skin and bone.

9

But if what is loved
is drawn away —
You saw the dead child
as he was given back to her.
You saw him leave
for his frozen world,
carried to its edge
in his father's arms,
the shapes of breath about him
pulled apart
and thinned
into the passing air.

Where he is
the soil stirs by him,
slanting his body
in a run of sand,
tamps him to itself,
lets go, and slides him again.
Casting above that,
the human eye seeks light
in what is shed
upon the world
and in the globe
where it resides.

So, grasped everyday
in a key-fob photograph,
or on a sideboard,
or pressed between pages,
he is immanent —
even soldered into marl
and the city's infill
he is imaginable.
What is in the mind
cannot be touched.
The lack of him
beats at the iron ground.

The stripe of light
we lie inside
carries me to you.
I can touch you,
pass from myself,
and in this accomplished
sentence: I love you.
With less — with what
is in the mind,
what is made possible
by the idea of him,
they love.

Five Winter Songs

Flower mornings
Of coldest winter
Remember my child
Born in the frost
Asleep in the frost

Cold December
Clear iron mornings
The sky from darkness
Pours down flowers
Made there for you

Remember my child
Born in the frost
Arm by his face
Stretched out he sleeps
Sleeps in the frost

Avenue of limes
Ignore the wind
Though you need breath
Keep still if you can
Let him sleep

Surprised by dreams
He turns and rises
And walks his room
Recognise his tears
Let him sleep

Avenue of limes
Cold as sealskin
Keep still
Though we cannot save him
Let him sleep

When that I see
The naked child
Fall to the grave
The tangled limbs
Of others laid

When that I see
The naked child
Losing her breath
Wounds upon flesh
Their life have kept

I ought to weep
If I any love know
As our passion moves
My love if I
Any love know

The winter rouses
All my grief
And feeds despair
From every hand
And feeds despair

The trees in grief
Their hearts display
Grand winter takes
With every hand
Deep in the love

Of his own demand
Arrogant thief
Arrogant thief
The winter rouses
All my grief

The slow-worm sleeps
So blindly coiled
And blest in blindness
Lightly laid
Survives the winter deeps

The fish in cold
Preserve their flesh
Living in latch
With the river land
They wait in winter's fold

Driving across
The lifeless night
The straight road freezes
Into light
Sleep my child my winter's loss

Sea Dreams

"I have seen enough of the obedient sea wave forever lashing the obedient shore. I find no emblems here that speak any other language than the sleep and abandonment of my woods and blueberry pastures at home."

Emerson, *Notebooks*

The sea imagines
That it loves the land
As fire loves flesh.
It draws the shingle
To itself, breath
On breath on breath.

It dreams within
Its sleepless mind
The dreams of stones
The dreams of fish,
The life of water
Dreamt away.

As fire would ravel
Flesh it comes,
This weight of dreams
Upon its back
And rages
For the folded land.

The sea imagines
That it knows its death,
And hauls it here,
The single labour
Of its mind, the loving
Burden of its breath.

17

The sea dreams
It will catch the air,
That weightless touch
Upon its back,
And draw it past
Their perfect seal.

Air leads the water
By its breath,
Hurt with its load
The staggered sea
Strives for that breath
The life above.

It waits for pause,
For the air's caress,
To bring it muffled
Through its weight
To the smothered body
Of itself.

Along their restless line
They lie,
The sleep of its death
Is the sea denied,
The joy of its life
The air forgets.

The dreams of the sea
Are its only life,
Flares in the cold
And wakeful deep,
Its shapeless mind
Destroys itself.

Closing its eyes,
The sea within,
The mind becomes
The sea enclosed,
Back and back
A wave in glass.

Dreaming itself
Into every breath
The smothered sea
Enfolds the mind,
The mind unshaped
Destroys itself.

Its shadows swim
Inside the sea,
The wave embraced
To its simple end,
All of its life
Is dreamt away.

The Swimming Body

I

In this world or out of it? —
The senses mostly muffled up for a while;
Or lapped in its elements,
Even this simple exemplary tank
Has the world's halves, and gives a line
To be followed, and followed.

I've pressed the goggles to my face,
Decided whether to jump or dive,
And now follow the line, breathing by the book,
Using the water as a pillow, rolling right
Behind the bow-wave, centreing to look
Straight in front, just below the surface,
The elbow high on entering, the hand palm down
Between shoulder and head, looking for it there,
Seeking its feel and its catch on the water
To draw movement from it.
Thinking on these things
Is enough for the mind,
Covered by this body, stretching with it
For its breath but with nothing more to do
With the world of air.

II

I am the first one there and stand looking
At the empty pool, still, bluish, and
Cleanly cut, its lines combed straight
To stay straight no matter
How the water shivers and rocks with swimmers.

The line of water and air too is still
And looks as if it would hold even if,
By an uncle's conjuring trick
The pool could be turned up,
No drop would fall to the ceiling.
To swim is to break and not break that line,
To cut it and leave it as you found it,
To love the old and simple world of water
And to need the air.

III

Imagine living in the deeps of this pool,
A silent, nearly signless world.
Imagine thinking that this is the world
You tread the surface of.
That shifting light above is somewhere else,
Maybe desirable, by turns brighter or darker,
With a shape sometimes flagging across;
But forever out of reach,
Whatever it may prove to be, — except
Once maybe, following some glint,
Neck stretched back, you kick upwards
And bob into this world.
And if you could hold the sight,
Would you recognise it as "purer
And more beautiful", true light
Shed freely, the true and proper place?
Or not bear the fullness of what you see,
And go again, twirl slowly away
Through the dense water and its thicker
And thicker green.

                   Though maybe you would sink
Gratefully, and see that this is the direction
We'd wish to go, that breaking the line
To truth, to heaven, to love,

We would find that they are simplicity, nothingness,
Lines.

      The tiles are sheer and meet with all their angles.
There is the blue of a good sky, or a lucent green.
It feels heavy, clothing, like a blanket;
It is quiet, and drawn over against the clamour
Carried in the shifting air.
We could live here if we could deserve it,
A simple utopia, a room cut from the ocean,
Regularised, oblong, uncomplicated,
No shadow or shade, unpocked
By inlets, creeks, seething tide-pools,
Any of the brocades and broideries of weed
That look only acted upon but are at work,
A thousand mouths, and nothing in that great
Voracity that cannot think but what it needs.
Here it is like the skull scoured out,
A white chamber, the bone shining like steel
And reflecting only itself.

IV

The mind as it lives with itself,
Noticing, taking things in, pondering,
Dismissing from its presence, allowing some things
To slip out, hit by recollection,
Looking forward (tonight, the summer),
Seems to float free, say, as I walk across
This park, just in front and a foot to the side.
Today there is a tune, some serious matter
For a while, bits of books, a meal,
An old friend in his gaberdine.
It can't keep to anything,
Its sentences are left open, it is a conversation
Of unfinished thoughts, unfinishable, but
Running, running, even as it thinks of itself
As itself, intelligence, consciousness,
"The life of the mind" — and here it might be pleased —
What else can the soul be?

I am on my way to swim, the mind alongside
As I say, moving briskly in the cold through
Some interest or other, spending some time
On what to do — how many lengths, in what pattern?
Re-running Salnikov, today's sports page:
A 100 in under a minute times 15!
Be solicitous but stern with the lungs
And the aching arm.

The trees in the park are shuttered.
A young man comes into view, his hair shaved up
Around his ears, his shoes laceless and without socks.
He is speeding round the paths turning
In sharp angles and shrieking as he goes,
A huge, strange call like a bird
From some land of marsh and cloud.
The mind has noticed this and is
Drawing back. If I pick up my pace,
Barely noticeably, we will be carried beyond him
As he arrives at the next corner and
Twirls on the ball of his foot towards us.
The mind is back inside, to the matter in hand,
No intention of being left to face a mind
Bodied out as this is in its dented and
Bundled flesh, its tiny running steps,
Strange curvets, and the wave beat of his cry
Pushing the air towards us. What
Comes down the path here, the vast chest,
The gait, the head, the face in white,
Is his mind, a physical thing as is my own,
Shrunk back now to be in step.

As the mind comes back it is not to prison
But itself. If I am not outside my body —
A foot to the side, a foot in front —
Neither is this body merely a house,
A space, a lodging, cavity, lathboard crack,
But something that is fluent in the mind,
As the mind itself is mortised
In this body's nervousness.

What the mind makes of anything comes of how
The body's made, as through the limb of sight,
Or what it touches and what touches it,
Like this water slipping past, happening
Outside the brain but not simply arriving there
To be noticed but already having joined us
At the skin. This is the border of the world,
The edge of space, the tireless lapping
Of the thought of truth, the pulse of death,
The simple outline of the self — here, and
Here, and here — the edge inventing the idea
Of itself
Of what it is and what it might be
Of what it is and what it might be
And so on and so on and so on.
Everything comes by the body and is streaked by it.

II

The Silver Eagle

Map tables of veined marble; state rooms; desks; clerks.
The Secretary of State comes in at three.
It is November: his aide puts on the lights,
Rinses his cup and saucer and lays them out.

War is to be detested for its savagery.
If cannons boom once more in the Medway towns
Think of the domestic misery that will ensue.
But men are happy; the brute world soluble.

A silver eagle perched on Wilhelm's beaver

A silver eagle melted from an inkstand

Shrieks

> *"No, that is not true!*
> *I warn you that is not true!"*

Three Poems on the Battle
of Jutland 1916

"After that we sent up shells with a message of hate . . . I could not sleep for the memory of the sights I saw that day . . ."

I / H.M.S. Invincible

Shoals of North Sea cod
Are interrupted by an Admiral
Swallowing their live water.
He dies screaming
In broad fathoms among
Coal shovels and scalded stokers
Suddenly washed of their dust.

The scrupulous historian tells
Of six survivors. One thousand
And twenty-one went
Scrambling down. The façade
Invincible, bow and stern,
Subsides: two hulks.

II / H.M.S. *Black Prince*

As night came,
the cruiser *Black Prince*,
steaming trustily in pursuit,
fell in with
the German fleet,
thinking them British.
The Germans, guilty of
no such error,
turned efficiently
to send her down.

Some of the men
floated for a while,
shouting to each other
among chewed boats and comrades.
None was saved.

III / *Summary*

A padre rescues a parrot
From plucked extinction.

Fisher shifts for his grave
But his dream just holds.

Brisk gunners, unhooded now,
Turn in their bunks with open eyes.

The sea resumes impatiently
Its measured swell.

Both sides claim victory.

The War with Japan

i.m. Percy Whiston, died 1944

In that last evening the hot glazed sea
By Java rocked then stilled, smoothing itself.
Luckless, sick of the prison ship, and un-
Serviceable as he now was, the boy died.

The sea rocked then stilled. Slowly he turned, as
Though in a hand, a figure gilding and
Decorating itself. He was consumed
There — all his life and loves — *"Abide with me!"*

Illusory Wars . . . 1914 . . . 1944 . . . 1984

"Lord Esher delivered lectures on the lesson of *The Great Illusion* . . . A twentieth century war would be on such a scale, he said, that its inevitable consequences of commercial disaster, financial ruin and individual suffering would be 'so pregnant with restraining influences' as to make war unthinkable."

"Tears came even to the most bold and resolute."

Barbara Tuchman, *August 1914*

I / 1914

Ambassadors, generals, secretaries for war
Have done so much to get themselves so far
And they weep. In the amber of Petersburg
Emissaries embrace; Churchill crosses the kerb

On the short walk to where he will cry,
Blubber, sob, melt like Monsieur Messimy
At the same hour in tears as he comes to speak,
His mind gulped suddenly by what will break.

Their fingers trace small pebbled lanes across
Glistening fields, past gardens with some trellis
Of clematis or vine, a corner for gooseberries,
The banging of a lattice door that carries

Over the way on the quickening wind.
As they inch on from Kovno to Ostend
They brush the Channel with their braided cuffs,
Thread the nations, and pull at handkerchiefs.

34

II / 1944

A water-butt has us clinging to its rim.
A boys' adventure would be to tipple in
Like frogmen, sound and swim the inkwell,
And fasten our charges to the *Tirpitz's* hull.

The triumphal generation of small boys
Play dead, go hand to hand from house to house:
My cousin, smithereened again, yet lives;
My uncle, tipped into a distant sea, dives

From the light forever; my father
On his leave lets his uniform lie like a
Dummy where it's fallen —
Meine familie ist alles jetzt gefallen.

But warned and circumspect we take due care
Of garden terrors, stay near to the door,
Our allotment, bit of waste ground,
Nation, saved for us, the back lawn *wunderkind.*

III / 1984

Un and *im* — unimaginable, unwageable,
Unprofitable, improbable — will
Keep us calm. Perhaps the dead of those wars
Only pretend: an infantryman clambers

From the sticky field, a sapper rises
From a roadside drain, like pearl-divers
Able seamen kick back to the sun
And bob by their children in the warm lagoon.

The nations, twined across every garden plot,
Are now so interlaced, so much in one boat
Together, their hulls bumping the ice
Together, both conquered, they shall embrace.

Acid-free pages turning in the breeze,
The histories of future fiction erase
The heavy lanes and the ministers who weep.
My son reads *Liquidate Paris!* as he drops to sleep.

III

Legal Crimes: The Nurse-Tree

Human dreams, worked up in the capable mind,
Phrased into flesh, come out and perform on earth, in air,
    in time,
. . . as with . . . this man: a handsome soul,
As evil as ourselves, silvered by imagination
To be our example, a tooth drawn
For sorcery, the token of a better age,
His light body flexed and hung
Out of the love we bear ourselves,
Love for the precious grave.

1815

I / *The Mill-Girl*

Above her face
Dead roach stare vertically
Out of the canal.
Water fills her ears,
Her nose her open mouth.
Surfacing, her bloodless fingers
Nudge the drying gills.

The graves have not
A foot's width between them.
Apprentices, jiggers, spinners
Fill them straight from work,
Common as smoke.

Waterloo is all the rage;
Coal and iron and wool
Have supplied the English miracle.

II / *Another Part of the Field*

The dead on all sides —
The fallen —
The deep-chested rosy ploughboys
Swell out of their uniforms.

The apple trees,
That were dressed overall,
Lie stripped about their heads.

"The French cavalry
Came up very well my lord."
"Yes. And they went down
Very well too.
Overturned like turtles.
Our muskets were obliged
To their white bellies."

No flies on Wellington.
His spruce wit sits straight
In the saddle, jogging by.

III / *The Important Man*

Bothered by his wife
From a good dinner,
The lock-keeper goes down
To his ponderous water's edge
To steer in the new corpse.

A bargee, shouting to be let through,
Stumps over the bulging lengths
Of his hatches,
Cursing the slowness
Of water.

The lock-keeper bends and pulls her out
With his bare hands.
Her white eyes, rolled upwards,
Just stare.

He is an important man now.
He turns to his charge:
The water flows uphill.

IV / *Death of the Mill-Owner*

Shaking the black earth
From a root of potatoes,
The gardener walks
To the kitchen door.

The trees rattle
Their empty branches together.

Upstairs the old man
Is surprised.
His fat body clenches —
Mortified
At what is happening.

The Mad Talk of George III
and A Hymn to Liberty

". . . A century that thinks about liberation and phantasises prisons . . ."

HANS MAGNUS ENZENSBERGER

I

The slow-worm from my orchard seeking me
Creeps to my counterpane and waits,
His body curled here in my linened hands.
I lift him up and wind him round
My temples like a tender vine
Bringing his head to rise so neatly from my brow.
He is the slender vessel of my power,
My man of justice, not the stricken silver
Of a Pharaoh's crown but moving flesh,
And able to embrace us all.

II

I sit alone in my chair on the bare moor,
The grass in flood in the orb I hold.
I sit as I did for anointment:
Attendants bringing up the coy canopy,
Archbishop Ambergris mounting the steps
To smooth my tousled head
For ministers to tell me their tales,
Doctors of the nerves, philosophers,
The black child of 'la liberté',
His eyes like scorched stones.

* * *

I sit alone in my chair on the bare moor,
Monarch of the yellow grass that laps my feet,
Of fearful space, a saucer of tussocks
And covert pools.
                    I cannot abide wildness —
Satan is the prince of open air.
His will incites the mobile grass beyond itself
And hurls the tidy song-bird round the sky.
He it is brings, bemused from his club of devils,
The black child of 'la liberté' —
The blackened child of 'la liberté' —
For me to reason with.

* * *

Caught in the romance of king and child,
I show the boy this man,
Put up to hang,
Dreamed out of us and labouring in the air,
Who swims for a moment, rests,
Swims, and then rests.
The earth cannot hold his stillness.

III

Candidus, my tall blood-prince, my grenadier,
Come with me since I love you.
Let us find a grove in middle Europe
Raised from sandy soil
Where the words will leave these stories
We have become and steal away,
Hallooing still one to another
Like accomplices on a dark road,
But gone.

                    And we can dissolve,

blushes into white space   forgetting even

        the moss of a tree

                        on its north side

the lost touch of it

A Hymn to Liberty

Count all the miner's hours, all his breathing
To the point of light.

A scud of air across the water's open face;
A child dabbles the flats of her palms
And laughs as she watches their play.
Each tree its silence breaks.

The movement of a breath of air across the lips
Creates the mind, and gives all of us our lives —

The inspired Republic,
A commune like the body with the air.

The child in love with the endless lake
Draws all her breath

The Garden Master

The gardener digs his trench for planting.
He uses stakes and old string for his line,
A riddle to take stones from his best soil.

His master pokes around, inquires,
Points with his stick but dare not interfere.
Later he finds his shears rusting in the long grass.

The redcurrant bushes should be moved today.
The hedges are only half-finished
And privet left lying will poison the soil.

But the gardener talks to a man
By the bottom gate, then leaves.
The master is able only to let it happen.

Several days pass by the untended garden.
The cook has to come out herself
To search for cabbages among the weeds.

The master, increasingly outraged,
Fumes after that neglectful gardener
And is expected to act soon.

Who was it last lived at the ruined cottage?
In your story the gardener met the miner,
Sat out the night, and did not go home.

No one saw hide nor hair of them again.
At length the furniture was removed —
Some sold in lots, some given away, some burnt.

Behind his walls, glass set in the top,
Behind his rows of trees, his rain,
His long garden now in rack and ruin,

The master lies, as though himself
Starched into his sheets, dying,
Though as he believes, only wintering.

IV

VI

Before Battle

Our precious earth has borne us on her breast all night.
We rise and leave her, embrace each lovely comrade,
And descend, like reapers to the battle place.

The cries that come and so break up the air dissolve.
Tomorrow dances on a field of peace,
Phlox, carnation, chamomile.
We wade so deep in our desire for good.

Thomas Müntzer

for David Spooner

Thomas Müntzer was a Protestant reformer in the early years of the German Reformation. He was a radical and a visionary both in theology and politics for whom religious thought and experience became integrated with ideas and movements towards social revolution.

Travelling through Germany, preaching and writing, continually in trouble with the authorities, he came to support and lead struggles by common people against the monopolies of wealth and learning. In 1525, in the Peasant War, he led an army against the princes which was heavily defeated at Frankenhausen. Müntzer was subsequently captured and executed.

> *Doubt is the Water, the movement*
> *to good and evil. Who swims on*
> *the water without a saviour is*
> *between life and death.*
>
> — Müntzer

> *I have seen in my solitude*
> *very clear things*
> *that are not true.*
>
> — Machado

I

Just above where my house sits on the slope
Is a pond, a lodge when the mine was here,
Now motionless, secretive, hung in weeds.

Sometimes on clear nights I spread my arms wide
And can fly, stiff but perfect, down
Over this pond just an inch above the surface.

When I land I have just one, two drops of water
On my beard. I am surprised how quick
I have become a flier, a walker on air.

II

I see my brother crawling in the woods
To gather snails' shells. *This is not
A vision.* Look carefully and you can tell

How he is caught in the roots of a tree
Whose long branches spread upwards bearing as
Fruit gardeners and journeymen, merchants

And lawyers, jewellers and bishops,
Cardinals chamberlains nobles princes
Branch by branch kings pope and emperor.

III

I feel the very earth is against me.
Night after night she turns in my sleep
And litters my fields with stones.

I lie out all summer spread like a coat
Over the earth one night after another
Waiting to catch her. And then

She is mine and the rowan blooms —
His black roots swim out and dive to subdue her —
His red blood cracks in the air and saves me.

IV

How many days did I search in my books
For such power, crouched like a bird under
My roof and lost to the world?

Scholars say God no longer speaks with us
Men — as though he has grown dumb, lost his tongue,
(Cut out for stealing a hare or a fish?)

Now I explode — out of this narrow house,
My mind lips hands skin my whole body
Cursing them for their flesh and their learning —

V

dran dran dran we have the sword — the purity
Of metal — the beauty of blood falling.
Spilt it is refreshed, it freshens also

The soil which when we turn it will become
Paradise for us once rid of these maggots
And their blind issue. They will seek about

And beg you: "Why is this happening to us?
Forgive us Forgive us", pleading now for
Mercy a new sweet thing they've found a taste for.

VI

So you see from this how I am — Müntzer:
"O bloodthirsty man" breathing not air
But fire and slaughter, a true phantasist —

"A man born for heresy and schism",
"This most lying of men", "a mad dog",
And all because I speak and say: God made

All men free with His own blood shed.
Hold everything in common. Share evil.
And I find I am a god, like all men.

VII

He teaches the gardener from his trees
And the fisherman from his catch, even
The goldsmith from the testing of his gold.

In the pond the cold thick water clothes me.
I live with the timorous snipe, beetles
And skaters, the pike smiles and moves with me.

We hold it in common without jealousy.
Touch your own work and the simple world.
In these unread creatures sings the real gospel.

VIII

I have two guilders for a whole winter.
I ask for company and food from beggars,
The very poorest, those I fancy most

Blessed . . . I am in love with a girl
And dare not tell her so . . . she makes me
Like a boy again — sick and dry-mouthed.

How often have I told you God comes only
In your apparent abandonment. This is
The misery of my exile — I was elected to it.

IX

My son will not sleep. The noise
And every moving part of the world
Shuttles round him, making him regard it,

Giving him — only four years old! — no peace.
He moves quietly in his own purposes
Yet stays joyless. There is no joy to be had,

And he knows that and is resigned to it.
At his baptism we dressed him in white
And gave him salt as a symbol of this wisdom.

X

I am white and broken. I can hardly gasp out
What I want to say, which is: *I believe in God* . . .
At Frankenhausen His promised rainbow

Did bloom in the sky, silky and so bold
No one could mistake it. Seeing it there
I thought I could catch their bullets in my hands.

An article of faith. I was found in bed
And carried here for friendly
Interrogation. They ask me *what I believe*.

XI

Their horsemen ride over our crops kicking
The roots from the ground. They poison wells
And throw fire down the holes where people hide.

An old woman crawls out. She is bleeding
And screaming so now they say they are sorry
And would like to bandage her. She won't

Go with them. She struggles free. *I see it
I see it* — she is bound to die . . .
This is the glittering night we wake in.

XII

I lie here for a few hours yet, clothed still
In my external life, flesh I have tried
To render pure, and a scaffold of bones.

I would resign all interest in it.
To have any love for my own fingered
Body and brain is a luxury.

History, which is Eternal Life, is what
We need to celebrate. Stately tearful
Progress . . . you've seen how I have wept for it.

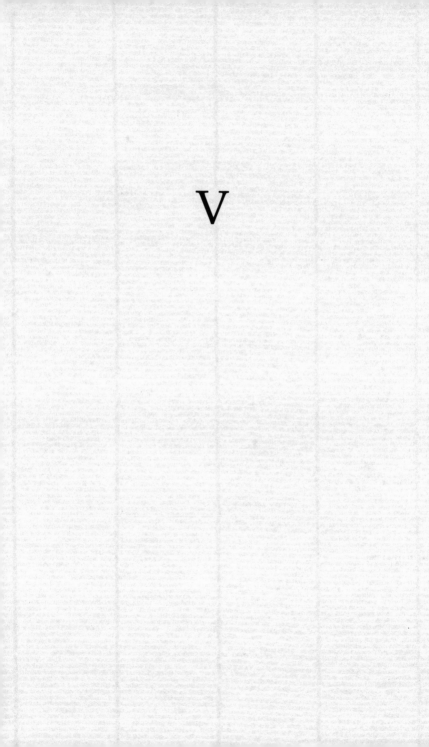

V

To His Lover

At the dead of night he breaks in upon her.

The room he knows so well,
That they have shared alike,
Is to him now the globe of his own eye
That he stumbles inside.

The bed-light flashes on and she is there,
She and some other friend, limbs thus and thus,
The sheet roped across them,
Pulled out of sleep.

— This is *love* he feels, something he *knows* he feels,
The best we can do, known to us by jealousy.

He leaves them, shoulders the laurel at the gate,
The wrought iron dragging at the paving stone,
And is back to the street,
Its heavy trees,
Pools of rigid light.

Sentimental Education

Delicatesse

Word of this 'revolution' drifts to us.
I sit, smoke, pore over papers
For the experts' views — though you distract me.
One can conjure whole suburbs, postmen,
Plumbers, flushed inelegant shopgirls
Ardent to be tearing up cobble stones.

What is all that compared with an eel stew,
Chicken, hard bread, and wine sharp on the tongue?
We eat ravenously, honest jagged knives
In our hands, the light of candles
Surrendering to your eyes. Ah my sweet,
To lose you will be such delicious sorrow!

The Ruin'd Abbey

A thousand years ago, the monks hereabouts
Would recognize early promise. There were
Openings for the right humility,
The sound contribution to scholarship.
Founded on such rock, juggler or jongleur,
There was no need to play with words.

I see you are not interested.
But where you sit to take off your shoes
Are tiles beautifully engraved with the Serpent
And the Fruit. Aware as I am of my own
Glibnesses, repetitions, minor faults, it is
A theme I never cease to contemplate.

The Forest of Fontainebleau

We admire the woodmen standing as we pass.
They sulk handsomely from the shoulders
Like beasts of the dark trees, wary of us.
One of them moves forward, and from a box,
Deliberately, staring straight into our eyes,
Produces three adders posed in his hands.

God knows it I am with you! all your trials
And your vexations and how you weigh them here
Bear upon me. But these your lithe spokesmen are
Too salutary, too quick. Show them to
Students, the educated poor, and tourists
Looking for something to amuse their friends.

Heart's Desire

heart

sleep   breath

desire   light

dream

If all this world were mine
From the ocean to the Rhine,
I could give up its charms,
To have the Queen of England
Lie here in my arms.
Anonymous, 12th Century German

One Love Poem

(after Lorca)

Oh, how hard it is
for us to love each other
at all!

For this love
the air, my heart, my hat,
hurt me.

And your eyes hurt,
you walk slower,
you wait, and go on.

How hard it is
for us to love each other
as we do.

The Day Comes

Lain close all night:
The moon a steady breathless sail.
The coming light
Is frozen out of air.

My love says it cannot be the day —
The light must deceive —
The lark, crying in the air
It loves, lies to us.

Daylight as thin as this
I wish would never come.
We are recovered from the dark
To part and walk about again.

The Tableau

We wake up into desire

A perfect tree
Light left to itself
Unruffled beasts
The sky and the earth
Embraced like friends
Us people
Clearly naked

Your slim tongue moves
Beneath my lip

Upon your handsome body
Is put the flesh
Of this desire

The Fierce Dream

I dreamt last night
A fierce dream
Of a tree
That in my garden grew,
But the garden became
A burying ground,
From the graves sleek flowers drew.

The summer so
Encased the air
It seemed we moved
In a golden bell.
But all the time
From the springing tree
The leaves and blossom fell.

The blossom I caught
In a yellow jug,
But that then slipped my hand —
Upon the flag below
A single sound.
Pearls and red drops
From all the fragments flow.

A dream so struck
From ragged sleep
Sucks out the redness
From the day.
The mind swoons to see again
How it contrives
Its own dismay.

Despair (Desesperada)

The day its steady breath conspires . . .
. . . we are caught in it.

Worse yet the heart is its ally,
Intending good, but involved.

It is incomprehensible —
More than any of us can embrace.

> *"Serene will be our days and bright*
> *And happy will our nature be*
> *When love is an unerring light*
> *And joy its own security."*

— if it is true
a passion for phrases does
dry up the heart
what then does silence do
desesperada?

> The day its steady breath conspires;
> We speak the speech of love and pain.
> We fight—to want our own desires—
> Our dealing hearts and flying brain.

Illumination

That is her lover lying there,
And she beside him lying close.
They do not speak, or move, or touch.
The lucid grass between them flows.

To lie, in stillness, breathing just,
Might motion time towards desire.
The air now barely moves the grass.
The sun in white draws off its fire.

Some Propositions
and Part of a Narrative

1. History cannot be grasped in the embrace of lovers.

2. There is love, but only as a little moment in their lives. History is untouched.

3. So it must be held that what history is, is how man deals with death, how he strives for a world where, at the last, death can be acceptable to all.

4. But not knowing history as we might, we seek a human lover — for the time being — to escape ourselves alone, to overlap one with another: "the body of me to all I meet or know".

. . . . as we left he said, "Sometimes it seems to me that every thought I have suspects the last."

A month later we saw the coachman again. He told us that one night the soldiers came back, broke their way in, and saying that he could not see anyway, took out his eyes. "It seems," he said, "I don't know who to please."

Love in the Arms of Death

Look at love in the arms of death,
So nearly won by his slender hands.
How he catches her rising breath
And robes her body where she stands.

He turns his head to weep for her
— His love is plain for all to see.
She finds within his touch a lover
Kinder than any man could be.

(* * *)

I wish for a strong heart
 As strong as sedge
Or reed or mallow grass.

I wish that this heart might
 Stare into water
And love what it sees.

The heart I want, so strong
 That it can bear
To love itself, loves you.

As He Found Her

She lay a long time as he found her,
Half on her side, askew, her cheek pressed to the floor.
He sat at the table there and watched,
His mind sometimes all over the place,
And then asking over and over
If she were dead: "Are you dead, Poll, are you dead?"

For these hours, each one dressed in its figure
On the mantelpiece, love sits with him.
Habit, mutuality, sweetheartedness,
Drop through his body,
And he is not able now to touch her —
A bar of daylight, no more than
Across a table, flows between them.

The Dead Come Back

The dead come back to us in dreams —
As we are told they do so they come.

Thus among the tablecloths and cakes,
The ham and sliced tongue and all the objects
Of this earth,
The company known and unknown at this latest funeral,
Lily, large and powdered in her flowery dress
Appears to her brothers and all of us
Like a star, a celebrity back among her own,
Nearly a sister again, nearly an aunt,
All of us parting for her, shy of touching
What we have brought to mind.

Unable as we are to die,
The dead come back to us in dreams —
As we are told they do, so they come.